CW01091238

Bound By My Choices
by Keshawn A. Spence

© Copyright 2018 Keshawn A. Spence

ISBN 978-1-63393-617-1

Published by

 köehlerbooks™

210 60th Street
Virginia Beach, VA 23451
800–435–4811
www.koehlerbooks.com

BOUND BY MY CHOICES

How a death nearly broke me but the Navy saved me

KESHAWN A. SPENCE

VIRGINIA BEACH
CAPE CHARLES

For my grandmother, Evelyn, my father, Francis, and Aunt Ruth and Uncle Orphus. In life, we lose so many loved ones that the list becomes endless. We must savor the memories, for those who have passed are forever with us, every step of the way, and watching over us. I thank God for the opportunity to have lived my life, and for surrounding me with people who have helped mold me into the man I am today. You will always be faced with choices that affect the rest of your life. Don't let your past mistakes define who you are.

Table of Contents

Prologue..1

Chapter 1
IN THE BEGINNING...7

Chapter 2
DAD'S FAMILY...13

Chapter 3
GROWING UP FAST...17

Chapter 4
A FATHERLESS AND MOTHERLESS CHILD................21

Chapter 5
MY SIBLINGS..32

Chapter 6
MEMORIES FROM THE COUNTRY.............................37

Chapter 7
SCHOOL DAYS..42

Chapter 8
A FATHER'S STRUGGLE: THE STORY OF FRANCIS...47

Chapter 9
MY MOTHER'S STORY...54

Chapter 10
RELATIONSHIPS..58

Chapter 11
THE ROAD TO SUCCESS...61

Chapter 12
BOOT CAMP...65

Chapter 13
ROAD LESS TRAVELED..70

Acknowledgements..77

About The Author..78

First CPO gathering as a Chief. Khaki Ball 2013, San Diego, CA.

Me as a young Third Class Petty Officer at my first command, VFA-203.

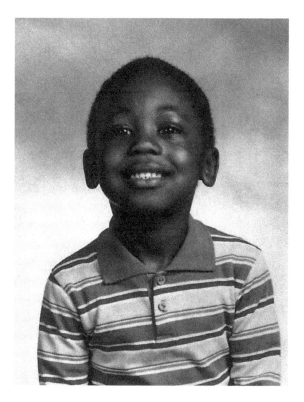

Me as a young child while being raised by my grandmom.

A photo of my dad from his funeral.

Me at Calvary United Methodist Church.

Me and my brother Keon at my Head Start graduation.

Community Relations Project, Building Homes for Habitat for Humanity in Kauai, Hawaii. August 2012.

USS Crommelin also known as "America's Battle Frigate,"
in port Pearl Harbor, HI.

Out at Sea in Hawaii but close enough to see the Waikiki shoreline.

Me standing on the pier in my dress whites.
USS Crommelin decommissioning ceremony, October 2012.

Me, my dad and son Josh at my college graduation for my bachelor's degree from Saint Leo University.

Fort Pierce, Florida with the real Captain Phillips from the Maersk, Alabama.

Haze Grey and underway. Somewhere out at sea.

Force Protection exercise in Pearl Harbor. That's me on the machine gun.

Seemed like the perfect day for a photo op.

My dad and brother sitting in the bleachers at my college graduation.

Me and my brother Keon.

My grandmother's grave site.

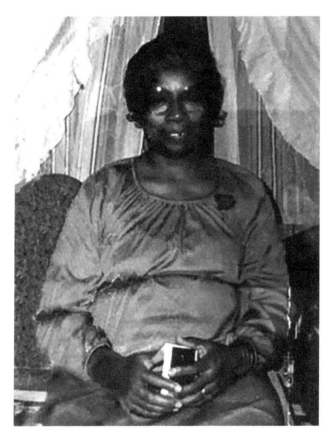

My grandma, Evelyn.

Bootcamp

Bootcamp

PROLOGUE

As I gazed out the window during the six-hour flight from Hawaii to San Diego, I began to contemplate the good and bad times I had experienced thus far. This was my fifth permanent change of station. Many different thoughts ran through my mind about what I wanted to accomplish next and what challenges lie ahead. I was excited to be off for a few weeks and wanted to see my family whom I hadn't seen for about a year or so. Although, I had been all over the world during my Navy career; there was no place like home with family and friends. Coming from humble beginnings, I never took that for granted. Where I come from you could be on top of the world one day and back down to the bottom on the next. The Navy had provided me with the long-term stability that I had been striving for during my childhood. Initially going in, I was just determined not to fail and become a better person than I was before I left.

I was fascinated with traveling to unknown territory and seeing the different types of national attractions and diverse groups of society. I had been flying on airplanes for at least ten years, but this flight transferring me to a new duty station was somewhat uneasy. Between the turbulence and my inability to fall asleep, this trip was different. I was transferring duty stations from the beautiful islands of Hawaii to sunny San Diego. I was no fan of winter and wanted to avoid a cold winter at all costs. I did miss my family on the East Coast but I was at the pinnacle of my career and needed to keep pushing forward. Wherever the Navy needed me is where I wanted to go.

During the flight, I was struggling trying to determine what my purpose in life was. Am I destined to become a Chief, an Officer, a lawyer or a politician? At this point, I was soul searching trying to determine my new area of focus. What about finishing college and joining the State Department as I had planned for several years now. That seemed like a more realistic goal. Become a Foreign Service Officer and work my way up to a position that positively impacted American diplomacy abroad. This was a great idea. Better than me sitting around waiting to win the lottery. For now, I just wanted to inspire someone to achieve their dreams. If I could make it from where I came from, maybe my story could motivate others to not settle for a predetermined outcome. If they say it can't be done, you prove them wrong.

I consider myself a critical thinker. I try not to base my decisions on impulse. I like to take calculated risks, which means I usually plan them out for weeks, months and sometimes years. I was and still am my worst critic. Even though I had experienced success in the military. I always longed for more. Every step of the way, I was determined to remain grounded and never forget where I came from. Writing a book about my life seemed to be a great way to capture both.

Many of my friends and family never made it this far. Some were called away to the kingdom of heaven. I was not only doing this for me, but for them as well. Despite my shortcomings, I felt that I had turned out pretty good considering my options. I still have a long way to go before I stop and pat myself on the back. This book is a reflection of me looking in the mirror and realizing my journey in life is far from over. The trials I experienced growing up will continue to fuel the man I am today. On the outside, people see an African American male, a devoted husband and father, a military senior enlisted leader, and a college graduate.

This memoir will peel back the mask of what you see on the outside. The road was hard with obstacles and challenges that defined who I am today. At times I wanted to give up and just fold and settle with mediocre achievements. I couldn't do it; my grandma wouldn't let me. One of her favorite poems was *"Don't Quit by John Greenleaf Whittier."*

> *When things go wrong as they sometimes will,*
> *When the road you're trudging seems all up hill,*
> *When the funds are low and the debts are high*
> *And you want to smile, but you have to sigh,*
> *When care is pressing you down a bit,*
> *Rest if you must, but don't you quit.*
> *Life is strange with its twists and turns*
> *As every one of us sometimes learns*
> *And many a failure comes about*
> *When he might have won had he stuck it out;*
> *Don't give up though the pace seems slow—*
> *You may succeed with another blow.*
> *Success is failure turned inside out—*
> *The silver tint of the clouds of doubt,*
> *And you never can tell just how close you are,*
> *It may be near when it seems so far;*
> *So stick to the fight when you're hardest hit—*
> *It's when things seem worst that you must not quit.*

When things got extremely difficult and I made mistakes, I would get on my knees and pray to God for help. For I was determined to create my own path.

"Do not go where the path may lead, go instead where there is no path and leave a trail." (Ralph Waldo Emerson)

FOOTPRINTS

One night a man had a dream. He dreamed
he was walking along the beach with the LORD.

Across the sky flashed scenes from his life.
For each scene he noticed two sets of
footprints in the sand: one belonging
to him, and the other to the LORD.

When the last scene of his life flashed before him,
he looked back at the footprints in the sand.

He noticed that many times along the path of
his life there was only one set of footprints.

He also noticed that it happened at the very
lowest and saddest times in his life.

This really bothered him and he
questioned the LORD about it:

"LORD, you said that once I decided to follow
you, you'd walk with me all the way.
But I have noticed that during the most
troublesome times in my life,
there is only one set of footprints
I don't understand why when
I needed you most you would leave me."

The LORD replied:
"My son, my precious child,
I love you and I would never leave you.
During your times of trial and suffering,
when you see only one set of footprints,
it was then that I carried you."

Chapter 1

IN THE BEGINNING

MY EARLY CHILDHOOD started in the countryside on the Eastern Shore of Maryland, in a small, backwoods neighborhood called Ironshire. It sat along a four-mile road on the outskirts of the town of Berlin. It was common to see cows, pigs, and corn and soybean fields throughout the area. I was raised by my paternal grandmother, Evelyn, in a one-story, single-family, three-bedroom home with an iron wood stove. My mother and father were both absent during my childhood, which was just fine by me. I hadn't developed a loving bond with either one and considered both of them parents by title only.

My grandmother raised me to go to church, and tried to develop me into a well-behaved young man. Every Sunday she would wake up and tune her radio to her favorite Christian radio station. One of her favorite songs was

"Rough Side of the Mountain." While singing her hymns along with the radio, she would cook a traditional country breakfast and expect me to get ready for church. Her normal breakfast menu would consist of pancakes, sausage patties, scrapple, and scrambled eggs with cheese. I could never forget the thickness of King Syrup she used to buy. God forbid you didn't take the syrup out of the refrigerator well before breakfast; it would be like frozen sap and take hours to pour from the bottle. You were better off eating your pancakes with butter only.

A young, stubborn kid, I did not always want to go to church. I would much rather stay at home and spare myself the stress of dressing up. The church was about a five-minute drive and well within walking distance. Like most churchgoers who dress up for Sunday services, grandma chose to drive.

The Calvary United Methodist Church congregation's youngest members were at least forty-five. Most were much older. I grew to enjoy the church environment once I actually made it inside. One of the highlights was attending Sunday school and learning about the Bible and the many blessings of our Lord and Savior. Not to mention the popcorn and juice Ms. Linda gave us each Sunday.

My friend Courtney and I were ushers, and took turns being acolytes. We would light the church candles before the service started and extinguish them when it ended. This kept us busy throughout the service, since we were typically the only kids, except for special occasions like Christmas or Easter when entire families attended. I don't recall the preacher's name back then, but I do remember some of the important members of the church: Mr. Harold, Mr. Preston and Mrs. Marion Smith, Mr. Chauncey, Mrs. Lula, Mrs. Sylvia, and the Young family.

My grandma and her sister, Aunt Thelma, were also important members of the church. My grandmother was the church secretary. The two were almost inseparable. Aunt Thelma lived across from my grandmother's house. She was strong willed, never afraid to speak her mind or advocate for old-school remedies instead of taking traditional medicine. Aunt Thelma once took out one of my loose teeth with a piece of string. She tied the string to a door knob, then she slammed it shut. It sounds harsh, but it was a fast process, and it worked.

Aunt Thelma was married to Uncle Floyd. He died in my pre-teen years. Uncle Floyd used to give me pieces of candy when I accompanied him walking on an adjacent road not far from my house. The walks were more like exercise for him, and probably a form of therapy. He refused to sit still and let Father Time creep up on him. He would always be outside doing something. As he continued to age, I believe he started to suffer from Alzheimer's disease. Through it all, Aunt Thelma always generously cared for him.

My grandmother and Aunt Thelma kept me in line until I was about thirteen years old. At my weakest moments, they found ways to make me laugh and take pressure off whatever messy situation I had gotten myself into.

Growing up, we only had three TV channels. There was no cable where I lived and certainly no Wi-Fi back then. You had to be rich to pay for cable lines in our neck of the woods. The only good thing about having three channels was that no one argued over what to watch, although my grandmother was obsessed with soap operas. The TV would show sports and movies most of the time, and PBS showcased *Sesame Street, Reading Rainbow, Mr. Rogers' Neighborhood,* and so forth. Two of my favorite PBS shows growing up were *Ghostwriter* and *Where in the World is Carmen San Diego?* Kids these days have probably never heard of these shows.

I remember watching the Duke Blue Devils play in the 1992 NCAA men's college basketball national championship. From that day since, I have always been a fan of the Duke Blue Devils. People often find that strange, since I grew up in Maryland and Duke resides in North Carolina. I am not sure how I became a Washington Redskins fan either, but I was used to rooting for them as a kid, since it was the closest team to my hometown. The Baltimore Ravens came many years later and are closer, but my loyalty remains with the Redskins.

In the country, we entertained ourselves by playing football and basketball in the backyard. We didn't have fancy basketball courts like many families in more upscale neighborhoods. Our basketball rim without a net was nailed onto a wooden backboard, which was either nailed into a tree or wooden pole. Occasionally, it would fall down after prolonged use.

When we were not playing outside, I would walk across the cornfield to my older cousin Junie's house, or my cousin Mark's. Junie had all the game systems: Sega Genesis, Nintendo, and Atari. I wasn't sure whether his mom, Ms. Geraldine, was spoiling him or he saved up the money to buy them himself. It was no coincidence that he was unbeatable on all the games he had. If you were lucky to beat him it was because he made a mistake, and that was not likely to happen twice. Junie also had all the cheat codes for all the games, such as Mortal Kombat, Mike Tyson's Punch-out, and Super Tecmo Bowl. He would let me borrow his Nintendo Power pad to play the track and field game. It was fun when you had others to play with, since I traditionally grew tired of playing Super Mario and Duck Hunt.

Cousin Mark had the coolest toys, which included remote-controlled cars and walkie-talkies, and a cassette stereo system. He lived with his grandparents as well. His grandmother, Ms. Mary, gave him anything he wanted. We were only a year apart in age, so we bonded really well. We used to have dunk contests on his basketball court. One time, I dunked, and had turned around to showboat my dunk when I felt the rim come down and hit the back of my neck. From that point on, I was cautious, never turning my back on the rim after a dunk. Once Mark moved from the country there wasn't as much to do, so things got pretty boring.

CHAPTER 2

DAD'S FAMILY

MY GRANDMOTHER HAD three girls and three boys. My aunts were named Ruth, Margaret, and Beatrice; my uncles were Levin and George. My father was named Francis.

Both Uncle George and Aunt Ruth preceded my grandmother in death. I never had the pleasure of meeting my grandfather, who died before I was born. I always wondered if my life would have been different if I had spent time with my grandfather. Most of the people I have met over time developed strong bonds with their grandparents. That was certainly true of my grandmother, who I regarded as my real mother.

My biological mother, Konya, was hospitalized shortly after I was born for reasons that remain unclear. I was told she was a victim of domestic abuse by my father. Both parents told contradicting stories about this situation. My mother's story is quite confusing. As I understand it, when I was seven months old my dad beat her and she lapsed into a coma. He never admitted to it, but I suspect there was some infidelity throughout the relationship on both sides.

I don't blame either one for my childhood. I'm actually quite happy they didn't raise me. When I was four, my mother showed up at my grandmother's and tried to force me to go with her. I was afraid, because I didn't know this woman who was pulling and tugging at me. I threw my shoes at her in an attempt to escape her grip. She was ordered to leave my grandmother's house. This was the point when my brother, Keon, permanently moved with her.

My grandmother was a nice Christian lady. She had retired from being a cafeteria attendant at the local high school. Many of the cafeteria attendants that were still employed with the high school when I attended spoke very highly of her and mentioned her often. Her name was usually evoked when I was doing something that she would not have appreciated or approved of. I don't remember hearing my grandma use any type of profanity—ever. On the other hand, I never took her kindness for weakness. I used to get suspended from the school bus for fighting, cursing or talking back in a disrespectful manner to the bus driver, and suspended from school for similar offenses. I would try to hide it from her by discarding the school notices that were mailed home, because I knew a whipping would be the consequence of my actions.

There were two old-school methods my grandmother used to discipline me—a belt or a switch (small tree branch). She would tell me to go get a switch; to her surprise, I would come back with the smallest branch I could find in hopes of reducing the whipping. That strategy only antagonized my grandmother, who would get a larger switch and intensify the whipping. She would spank my rear end, and I usually tried to put up a good defense for a short while, crying and using my hands to block the swats, until she chose to intensify her spanking. After a few good swats, she would stop and ask if I had learned my lesson, and warn me not to repeat the conduct that got me in trouble or else I would see the same fate.

As I continued to mature into adulthood, I grew to appreciate the discipline she tried to instill in me. Kids are lacking that nowadays, and many have seemed to lose respect for their parents and elders.

Grandma Evelyn was the type of person that would give you the shirt off her back if you needed it. She was always willing to lend a helping hand with food or money, and instilled in me to treat others the way I wanted to be treated. It was clear that she was thankful to God for every blessing that he gave us. She never wanted to see anyone suffering or go without food or shelter.

As an incentive for reading books under the "Book It" program, kids would receive a free, kid-size personal pan pizza. She would drive thirty-plus miles each way to take me to get the pizza, which always put a smile on my face.

Every year, she purchased my school clothes from different department stores and never relied on my parents to provide anything. When I was a kid, there was no Walmart or Target; we only had Roses and Kmart. Believe it or not, jeans were relatively inexpensive compared to today, and there was little demand for designer brands, at least not where I lived. Back then, gas was still around 99 cents a gallon.

My grandmother was the best thing that happened to me. To honor her, I have a tattoo on my left arm that reads: *She will never die. She lives through me.*

Growing up, Grandma Evelyn always told me I needed to learn how to cook because she would not be around forever. I had no idea what she was talking about at the time. That truth descended on June 17, 1995. She lost her battle with cervical cancer and the Lord took his angel home. This marked the beginning of my young adolescence, which was about to spiral out of control.

CHAPTER 3

GROWING UP FAST

WHEN MY GRANDMA DIED, I was traumatized. I would crawl under my bed and cry for hours, asking God to bring her back. I had watched her lose her hair from chemotherapy and always hoped and believed that she would get better. I remember holding her hand in the hospital, and during her final days. She would always smile, despite feeling deathly ill. As a kid, I would sit next to her rocking chair, and she would rub my head while singing gospel hymns. Nothing could have prepared me for her death. If it were up to me, she would have lived forever.

The day she died, our family was coming home from an amusement park in Ocean City, Maryland, named Jolly Rogers. Despite the fun we had during the day, the news we received made us forlorn. The memories of her flooded my brain. She had been there for me for as long as I could remember. Despite growing up with marginal income, she always made sure I had everything that I needed and much of what I wanted. This included a Nintendo game system, when it was still popular, and decent school clothes and shoes.

My favorite games were Duck Hunt and the first Super Mario Bros game. She bought all my birthday and Christmas gifts. I don't remember my parents ever getting me anything for Christmas. It was common to not hear from either of them on holidays and birthdays.

When I was ten, I got hit by a truck while riding my bike on the road near our house. Sadly, it was my fault, based on a gut reaction to change lanes. The accident occurred back in the era when the rap group Kris Kross was popular and kids would wear their clothes—shirts and pants—backwards. At the time of the accident, I was dressed like the hip-hop rappers I admired. My cousin Mark and I idealized Kris Kross back then, as did so many kids in my age group, listening over and over to the songs "Jump" and "Warm It Up."

I had just left Mark's house and was about two minutes from my house when I noticed a car tailgating me. It felt as if they were going to run into me or force me off the road. I got nervous and switched to the oncoming traffic lane. I did not realize that the left lane I was switching to turned into a blind curve. I was struck by a pickup. My bike and I were sent flying to the opposite side of the road, ultimately landing in a ditch bank. I remember seeing the sky for several seconds. Then I realized I was lying in a ditch. The driver of the truck stopped and tried to assist. I don't remember his name or what he looked like.

Eventually, my grandma and Aunt Thelma were at the scene of the accident. I felt pain, but the Lord took most of it on his shoulders. I had a severe cut on the left side of my stomach and one on my left thigh. As I looked up to the sky, I remember that I kept saying "I don't want to die." The ambulance took me to Peninsula Regional Medical Center in Salisbury, which was about thirty minutes away—the same hospital where I was born. The accident could have been the end of my life at such an early age, but God had a plan in store for me.

After evaluating me, doctors determined there was no major muscle damage to my stomach, but I was beat up enough to spend four days in the hospital. The huge gash on my stomach required staples to close it up. A catheter was inserted so I could urinate without getting up. Had I been awake when they inserted it, I would have negotiated for a better alternative. The catheter took some getting used to. When it was removed, the pain and aftermath were unbearable. The doctors thought it would be a good idea for me to immediately start walking around the hospital. I felt bad for the janitor that followed after me. I still remember the pain.

Life-changing experiences like these often bring strangers around you. There sat my mother and father in the same room. That was probably the first time I had ever seen them together. The young child in me pleaded for them to get back together for my sake—what a dumb idea, but at the time I was asking from the heart. Both of them looked at me as if I were crazy and still under the influence of anesthesia. Of course, it didn't work, but at least they were able to sit in the same room and be civil. The next time they were in the same building was my high school graduation.

After I got out the hospital, I had to be monitored for a week to ensure I was sufficiently recovering. My grandma decided to let my mom watch me during the week while she was working, an easy alternative because my mother apparently was unemployed. I'm glad it was only for a week or so. My mom would yell at me to walk straight and stop leaning toward the hurt side of my body. I don't think she comprehended the severe pain I felt, or that the staples in my left side limited my range of motion. This was the first time I witnessed how meanly she treated my brother. Keon was three years older than me and had lived with my mom for as long as I could remember. I knew from that point on that I never wanted to stay with her, and the time we spent together while I mended was too long.

CHAPTER 4

A FATHERLESS AND MOTHERLESS CHILD

AFTER MY GRANDMA DIED, I was reluctant to move with either one of my parents. There were multiple reasons preventing me from living with either one. I kept asking myself, *Why now?* They hadn't tried to raise me or play a significant role in my life thus far. I was very suspicious and unwilling to give them the opportunity.

Growing up, my grandmother always kept extra food in her car trunk, because if she brought all of the food in the house, her adult sons would eat up everything without a means of replacing it. Normally it was just me and my grandma living there. On separate occasions, my dad, my aunt Ann, and Uncle Skip would move in.

My aunt Margaret, who was called by her middle name, Ann, was the first to volunteer to take care of this stubborn kid mourning the loss of his grandmother. We stayed in my grandmother's home with my uncle Levin, who went by the name Skip. Aunt Ann had two adult daughters, Carlotte and Lonnie, whom I would talk to from time to time. They inspired me; both had good jobs and personal success stories.

At that point in my life, no one could tell me anything because I didn't want to listen. I was a rebellious thirteen-year-old, angry over the loss of my grandmother. I would pick and choose what things I wanted to do, regardless of what my aunt or uncle said. Nevertheless, they were patient and took good care of me.

Aunt Ann was a great cook, well known for her pepper-steak and chicken-divine recipes. She would always find hobbies to keep her busy, like crossword puzzles and crocheting. Although not very talkative at times, Aunt Ann tried her best to provide me with structure. She volunteered me to participate in the Assateague Island beach cleanup event that was sponsored by her employer. It was actually fun going to a beach state park, picking up trash and debris while watching the wild ponies and enjoying the breeze from the beach.

One Christmas, Aunt Ann decorated a Christmas tree with chocolate ornaments and decorations. Keon ate all the chocolate and blamed it on me. To this day I don't eat much chocolate. Ultimately, my aunt gave up because I was an unruly child, and moved out. She left me there with Uncle Skip. Aunt Ann had raised her kids; I was not her responsibility.

Uncle Skip was cool but not a model parent. There was never much food in the house. He would walk around the house and eat and drink everything in sight all day and night. Skip was one of the old guys who swore up and down that he knew everything. Whether something happened in the news, or the subject was a new invention or just a matter of life experience, it was pointless trying to argue with him. He never conceded a point, and would keep trying to convince you that he was right and you were wrong.

There were many days I would come home from school to a dark house because the electricity was shut off due to unpaid bills. Uncle Skip didn't have steady employment, just small handyman jobs here and there. For some odd reason, he thought he was a mechanic, but the truth of the matter was that he was far from it. Anything he took apart to fix was sure to never work again. This went for cars like his Buick, which is still probably sitting on bricks in the backyard, alongside a broken-down riding lawnmower. The term we used for so-called mechanics was "jack-leg mechanic." If someone was identified by this term, you knew not to trust them.

Sometimes Uncle Skip was a cook in a restaurant; other times, he would be in the forest chopping down trees to sell firewood. After Thanksgiving, we would eat turkey sandwiches for the next few months. I am not sure why Uncle Skip ended up in the predicament he did. He had been in the Navy and the Air Force. He was about five-foot-eight and had a lot of ailing bones and screws in his wrists.

He and Aunt Pam were married during my childhood and separated sometime after. I don't think either one ever filed for a divorce.

I lost track of how many kids Uncle Skip had. Besides the ones I grew up with, more seemed to sprout each year, but none of them lived in the house with me. All of his kids either stayed with their mother or were full grown adults. I don't recall ever meeting Julie and Jody, who were his twin girls. I grew up knowing some of his other kids: Levin Jr., Cezar, Lorikeet, and Simalene. I could never forget my cousin Jermaine, rest in peace. He died in his teenage years after a car accident. Throughout it all, Uncle Skip remained strong.

While living with Uncle Skip, my aunt Candy, my dad's sister, provided me with a cooler to keep snacks and goodies in, including my favorite blueberry muffins. After a while Uncle Skip became frustrated with me, so I moved in with Aunt Candy, which was a big improvement.

Aunt Candy was a heavily-involved church woman with a good heart. I always considered her old fashioned. She is the only woman I knew who could make a hundred dollars last an entire month. I think she is the reason I still prefer to go to yard sales to this day. One of her daily rituals was to keep her living room television fixed on the TBN network, which was a twenty-four-hour gospel network. It was like pulling teeth to get her to change the channel. It is easy to conclude that any kids that went over to her house resorted to playing outside.

My grandma lived with Aunt Candy during the final months before she was called to heaven. Aunt Candy was one of the nicest and most loving women you would ever meet, unless you were disrespectful or cursed in her house or around her. She had three sons, Morgan, Rashawn and Deshawn. These boys could do no wrong in her eyes. Morgan and Deshawn were natural outdoorsmen who liked to fish and hunt for rabbit and deer using guns or bows and arrows. I never had a hunting license, but I would go into the woods with them from time to time to shoot. I had to learn how to hold a weapon. Candy's sons would display their hunting prizes stuffed and mounted on their bedroom walls like trophies. They would skin their prey right in the backyard as if it were as easy as brushing their teeth.

Rashawn suffered from a mental disability, but he was as tough as they get. He would throw stuff at you and thump you upside the head when his mom wasn't looking. As kids, we tried to stay on his good side because he never got caught acting up. He would also use select curse words when his mom wasn't listening. Besides that, he was a great cousin and loved watching *Dukes of Hazard* and *Knight Rider*. Both shows were very popular during this time. Rashawn also loved to assemble model cars. God forbid if you went into his room or touched one of his cars without permission; he would have a fit.

I think I learned my motivation for cutting grass from Rashawn. He loved to cut grass; it was as if he were at peace and could not be bothered with anything else. After cutting grass, his only request was to get a cheesesteak sub. Shawn loved cheesesteak subs and so did I. Boomers, a hometown restaurant, had the best subs around thanks to Mrs. Renae. Aunt Candy was also a great cook. Her chicken and dumplings would have you asking for seconds and a to-go plate. During the summer, she would make homemade ice cream and sell it to neighbors. Her vanilla and strawberry ice cream was the best I have ever tasted. Most of our family holiday gatherings occurred at her house. The family united there, in part, to enjoy Aunt Candy's great food and fellowship.

My living arrangements with Aunt Candy also began to suffer due to my lack of discipline, and because of a bad influence: Aunt Candy's youngest son, Deshawn. As a teenager, I wanted to be just like him—working and having money, a car, nice clothes and pit bulls. Deshawn had three-wheelers, dirt bikes, different rifles, you name it. He taught me a lot about music, maturing as a teenager, and how to interact with women. We would often hang out partying and drinking into the wee hours of the morning, well after my curfew. My Aunt Candy tried her best with me, but as she would often say, I was getting "too big for my britches." She finally had enough.

The next stop on my journey was moving in with my sister Konya. For some reason, my mom thought it was cool to name my sister after her. I didn't have the opportunity to get to know much about my sister growing up because she didn't live with us. She was heavily into cosmetology and used to do my grandmother's hair. So, I would see her from time to time, but that was about it. Upon moving in with my sister, it was clear that she needed a babysitter for my first-born niece, who was named after her father. Truth be told, that may be the only reason my sister entertained such an arrangement. We had a unique relationship, I would say. At times, she acted like a controlling mother, which I definitely could not abide. Other times she was relaxed.

I started to develop a close friendship with Konya's boyfriend, Teon, who was also my stepbrother. Teon taught me how to ride dirt bikes, and we would always find some place to go riding and hang out and have some fun. During my time at my sister's, I was introduced to Ms. Shirley, one of Teon's aunts.

Ms. Shirley was one of the nicest devout Christian ladies I have ever met. She was another person that would give you the shirt off her back or the last coins in her wallet. When I needed a ride from work, she would always be there for me if she wasn't in church. I used to watch her son, DL, when she went to afternoon or evening church services. I didn't mind it at all because her house was fully stocked with food, snacks and any drinks or treat you could think of. DL had it made. She would also buy a pizza or something for dinner for me before she left. Ms. Shirley didn't have to pay us at all because she had cable, and cabinets stuffed with food. DL had a lot of energy and loved to run around; he hardly ever sat still, which I attributed to all the candy and snacks he consumed.

A few months later, I moved in with my cousin Deshawn and his girlfriend, Brandy. They treated me well, and I always had fun when they were around. We used to play cards and various board games. Brandy was Caucasian and very outspoken, regardless of who was around or how they might react. Her mother owned a restaurant in Ocean City, so it appeared that she grew up spoiled. Regardless, she cared about the wellbeing of others. From her, I learned how a girlfriend was supposed to treat her boyfriend. Brandy and Deshawn shared a bond that stood the test of time. Deshawn once had criminal charges filed against him for getting into a fight with Brandy's ex-boyfriend and knocking him unconscious.

I briefly worked as a dishwasher at Brandy's mom's restaurant. The family's relationship with me soured when Deshawn used me as a cover to hide the fact that he stayed out all night partying. He told Brandy that he had been out looking for me all night into the early morning, and that was the reason he had come home so late. The truth was that we were together the entire night hanging out in Ocean City. I stayed out and he needed an excuse to justify doing so. Brandy accepted Deshawn's lie and told her mother the same. Her mother, and Aunt Candy, and a family friend, Mrs. Beverly, who was a cook at the restaurant, each chastised me. They were under the assumption that I was not grateful for the opportunities that were provided to me. Instead of telling the truth, I chose to remain loyal to Deshawn, and vouched for his alibi. I soon moved out of Brandy and Deshawn's house as a result.

After running out of family members to take me in, I stayed briefly with one of my friends and his family. The Duffy family took me in as if I were one of their own. I owe a lot to Mrs. Judy, Ira, Julius, Vashon and Sheena. They made me tougher, and I truly witnessed the power of family. If one ate, we all ate. Mrs. Judy was heavily involved in church but didn't force us to go. Ira, Julius and I had so much fun. We pretty much did what we wanted, and rode up and down the streets with the speakers blasting. During this time, I purchased a 1989 Dodge Shadow. It had a lot of miles, but I was happy just having transportation. Eventually, the transmission broke and it cost me $550 to fix.

One afternoon I made a terrible decision of taking my eyes off the road to change the track on my portable CD player. When I looked up, I had a split second to slam on the brakes, which still resulted in me rear-ending a car in front of me. Luckily no one was injured, but my car was damaged beyond repair. I believe I ran into the back of a large SUV. The front of my car was smashed. The timing could not have been worse. It was a week before high school prom and I already had my date and tuxedo lined up. Now I lacked transportation. Being without a car was brutal in the area I grew up in. There should be a saying: "So goes the car so goes the friends." One of my cousins let me borrow his car to attend prom that year. He came to the prom and wanted his car back before the event ended, leaving me without a way to get my date home. Thankfully, she was able to get a ride home from a friend, and so was I.

One Saturday, I woke up in the house to loud knocking on the door. To my surprise I was the only one home. I opened the door and it was the county sheriff. We were being evicted due to unpaid rent. I didn't know what to do at this point, so I grabbed my belongings and left before I was thrown out. I made some calls at the pay phone and wound up moving back in with my sister.

My independence started to flourish when my sister moved to Wilmington and left me in Berlin. She found a job out of state and would commute back and forth to Berlin from time to time. She left me to maintain her apartment while she was away. To me that translated into her giving me my own place to stay. I was finishing up high school at the time, and was old enough to not need supervision. This was by far one of the best gifts that she could have given me. Me and my best friend, Larry, would always have company over and hang out and have a good time. We kept the place clean and it became the chill spot for the select people we would invite over. This was my first experience of completely living on my own and not having to answer to anybody about where I was going and when I was coming home.

The lease on my sister's apartment eventually expired and then I packed my bags and headed out, destined to find somewhere else to stay.

Chapter 5

MY SIBLINGS

I WAS BLESSED WITH having two sisters, Konya and Faren, and two brothers, Keon and Teon. Keon and I have the same mother and father. Konya has a different dad and Faren has a different mom. We all grew up mostly separated from one another. Teon is my stepfather's son, and therefore not blood kin. But we always viewed each other as true brothers. All of my siblings with the exception of Faren are older than me.

Keon's first name is Francis after our father, but he goes by his middle name. He's six-five—a giant—and has pretty good basketball and football skills. I always looked up to him, literally and figuratively. I'm only six feet tall.

Keon's athletic skills far surpassed my own and were better than most Division I college athletes. He played basketball and football in high school, but had little interest in college. Yet he was very talented. During his young adolescence, he could draw and sketch anything flawlessly just by looking at it. He won first-place ribbons in elementary and middle school, which he probably won't admit to. Not many people possess the talent that he has drawing.

Keon has four kids, three girls and one boy. He is one of the strongest people I know, having experienced a troubled past growing up with our mom, dealing with all her husbands and being shot with a firearm on separate occasions. I thank God that he is still here. He is the only one that can truly relate to the struggle of growing up with two dysfunctional parents and making something out of nothing. We often reminisce about how we were raised and all the adversity that we had to overcome. It is clear that we both went down different paths to ensure our children would be raised in a better environment than we had. Keon chose to find a job and work his way up until he found something he liked doing. We also grew up very competitive when it came to sports, and always wanted to win regardless of whose team we were on.

My stepbrother, Teon, is six feet tall and was also a basketball star. His on-the-ball defense is one of the toughest that I have ever seen. He has always been in my corner no matter what. I can talk to him and Keon about anything. He schooled me a lot about growing up on the streets of a small town and how to keep a tight circle of friends. Whenever I went anywhere with him, it was guaranteed that I was going to have some fun and meet some women.

When I got in trouble at school, he was the voice of reason. I remember our trips to Crisfield and hanging out in the projects. We would go to high school basketball games where the bleachers were packed. He is the one who introduced me to my first drive-through beer store. Wherever I went with him I was treated as family.

Teon's father, William, married my mom. Just like my father, William had problems with drugs and alcohol. William used to always tell me, "Never let a woman clock your money." I assume this was his way of talking about my mom and their marital problems. Will always talked to Keon and me about how much he loved his kids, but he was also an absent father.

My sister Konya looks just like our mom. They often share the same attitude, although Konya was raised by her father's mother. My oldest niece is a spitting image of little Konya. My sister hustles no matter what she does. Her primary trade is as a hair dresser, and she is very good at it. She is the only person I know who can work multiple jobs, do hair on the side, and still pretend to be broke. Even though we don't always see eye to eye, I know she cares for me deeply in her own special, stubborn way. She has three kids—two girls and one boy.

Faren is my younger sister. We share the same father. We were isolated during our childhood and never really got to know one another. This was mostly due to our parents not getting along. I actually liked her mother.

When Keon and I were kids, Faren's mother was somewhat nice to us. I remember she would take turns cleaning our ears out with peroxide and a bobby pin. Her mother did kick me out of their apartment once, when my dad was at work. It didn't bother me much because at that time I was still living with my grandmother. Faren is a great artist and has the same drawing aptitude as Keon. Somehow the drawing gene skipped me. Faren has one son.

I credit my cousins with helping me become the man I am today. I could take the time and talk about all of them, but it would take too long and no doubt be confusing because of my splintered family. Even so, I need to mention a few.

My cousins Carlotte and Iva taught me how to play card games such as Spades, Tonk and Speed. I have to give them props to my Spades success. My cousin Lonnie was the first one in our family to graduate college. That inspired me later on after my high school years. If it wasn't for that, I would have not realized there were goals worth achieving after high school. Carlotte also showed me that hard work and dedication enables you to take care of six kids and still be happy. She would say the constant supply of Pepsi soda also helped her cope. My cousin Nic showed me life outside of the countryside, since he lived in Washington, DC. When I stayed with him for the summer, I would get to watch *The Box* and see all the music videos, and watch him

DJ on the turntables. He gave me the motivation to want a house one day. My cousin Morgan taught me what not to do and to learn from his mistakes. He is probably one of the reasons I chose to have kids later on in life. Seeing him jailed for unpaid child support provided a valuable lesson in being responsible once you do have children, a choice I therefore postponed until I was older.

CHAPTER 6

MEMORIES FROM THE COUNTRY

EVEN TO THIS DAY I consider myself a "country" person. That's what it felt like where I grew up, in my grandmother's small, three-bedroom home surrounded by corn and soybean fields. During the summer months, the fields bloomed with crops. We children had fun running through the fields as a shortcut to get to our cousins' houses. We played kickball in the front yard and basketball and football in the backyard. Back then, it was mandatory for kids to play outside during the daytime. We were forbidden from running back and forth inside the house. Once you went out, you stayed out, and could run until your legs gave out.

Occasionally, we'd get a glass of Kool-Aid or simply drink from the water hose. When it was really hot outside, we would pour Kool-Aid into ice trays and then freeze it. We never really knew what the grown-ups were doing inside the house, and we didn't ask. I would often play in the woods and run around different areas that we called stages 1, 2, and 3. It was a simple way of keeping track of how far we were away from home.

In the country, it was common to see clothes hanging from a clothesline outside, just blowing in the air. We had a washing machine, but the country air was our dryer. During the summer, we would also stockpile chopped wood in the shed for the winter. The wood was a lot cheaper during the summer months when demand was low.

The summer was a good time to go crabbing. One of my grandmother's cousins, whom I called Aunt Veenie, loved to take us crabbing in Newark, Maryland. It had great locations for crabbing along remote tidal waterways off country backroads. We used chicken drumsticks as bait, tying them to the end of a rope and attaching a weight to the line so the drumstick would submerge. Crabs loved chicken for some odd reason. All you had to do was be patient and wait until your line started to dangle in the water. You would then pull your rope up nice and slow, trying not to lose the crab attached, and scoop them in your net. We would repeat this process until we caught enough crabs for a meal, or we ran out of bait.

In the summer, my cousins from Baltimore and Washington would come to visit. We had so much fun playing games and going to the beach in Ocean City, a major resort town and main tourist attraction during the summer.

We would ride go-karts, water rides at Jolly Rogers, or frolic at the inlet arcade and amusement park. The smell of Fisher's popcorn and Thrasher's French fries would make you stop in your tracks and buy some. And you couldn't leave the boardwalk without sharing a funnel cake.

The boardwalk was always packed during the summer. It amazed me during the winter that this resort town would be nearly empty with the exception of the locals. Ocean City provided summer employment for the majority of people within the surrounding areas. If you couldn't find a place to work in Ocean City, you didn't want a job. People traveled from overseas to seek summer employment.

One of my favorite jobs in "OC," as we locals call it, was working at Papa John's. When I was fourteen, I got a job at Domino's Pizza in Berlin. This was back when you had to obtain a worker's permit and abide by the rules. I worked there for a year or so and grew to like it.

My store manager, Ken Fitzsimmons, was a great leader and motivator. He took a chance and saw my potential, giving me my first on-the-books job. I tried my hardest not to let him down. He taught me about discipline on the job and how to push through tough circumstances, like when we were understaffed and the computer screen was loaded with pizza orders and the phones kept ringing. He instilled in his workers the fight to work through it with a smile and continue to produce great quality product that we could be proud of. Ken was about to make a move to Papa John's and offered to bring me and another skilled worker, my friend Tony, with him. We received a pay increase and a new storefront location in Ocean City. It was crazy to witness how drunken people acted while trying to order a pizza. I considered my pizza-making skills to be the best on the Maryland Eastern Shore.

As a pizza maker, I was pretty cocky. My friend Tony was a better pizza topper and overall faster to get the pizza in the oven. Who could have known at that point that we would both be able to rise up the ranks to become assistant managers? The skills I learned there served me well in future occupations. One big lesson was that it took teamwork to get the job started and to complete the mission. I had performed various odd jobs prior to my long stay with Papa John's, such as dishwasher, carpet installer, and prep cook. Nothing was more rewarding than the knowledge and skills that I learned from Ken during my three years working at Papa John's.

The work was mostly during the summer months since the winter was too slow for business. After relocating to Delaware for close to a year timeframe, I was hired to work as an assistant manager at Papa John's near the University of Delaware. It was a good job, but there were different dynamics that I had to adjust to in moving from a Papa John's in a resort town to one in close proximity to a college. Overall, the staff was very welcoming, but I long missed being on the Eastern Shore. I later quit my job because the manager tried to suspend me from work after I failed to attend a management training course. I explained to him that I was too old to be suspended, so I quit and walked out. I came in a few weeks later to pick up my final check and never looked back.

Chapter 7

SCHOOL DAYS

WHEN I WAS A CHILD, I enjoyed attending school. The Head Start program gave me my first impression of a schoolhouse setting. I don't recall any of the learning activities, but I do remember playing outside on the bikes with other kids, and that my uncle Orphus worked there.

I attended Buckingham Elementary School, which provided me with a great foundation to build upon. The elementary school was for kindergarten through fifth grade. I'll never forget my kindergarten teacher, Ms. Raine. She was one of the nicest ladies I have ever met. She truly cared for her students. I didn't get into much trouble in elementary school, but I remember my fourth-grade teacher, Mr. Booth, breaking yardsticks across students' desks. He was a real terror, and used fear tactics to keep the students in line. I was recommended to attend enrichment lab with Ms. Kuhn, and I enjoyed it. I learned many diverse things: the different types of whales, Greek mythology, and about Jacques Cousteau's explorations of the sea. Elementary school was also where I developed a desire to play four-square and dodgeball. Even in those days, I was very competitive. We were introduced to gymnastics, but I never really got into it.

After elementary school, I attended Berlin Middle School, which was for grades six through eight. In middle school, I started to get into little scuffles here and there. This is where I started to become a class clown, and rebellious. I would get suspended from school for fighting and so forth, in-school detention for being disobedient, or banned from riding the school bus. Middle school was fun despite my shortcomings.

I enjoyed keyboarding class, which taught me how to type using games such as Oregon Trail. Believe it or not, it was a lot of fun back then. Kids in this day and age probably have never heard of it. I also participated in wrestling club, which was fun. I kind of wish I had stuck with it over the years.

Coach O'Halloran was the wrestling club coach as well as the physical education teacher. Overall, he was nice with a tough-guy demeanor. As long as you got dressed to participate in gym activities, he was fine. It wasn't until seventh grade that I learned what a layup was in basketball. I was well behind the athletic curve.

In middle school, one of my teachers, Mrs. Friedman I believe, informed me that I was potentially a male chauvinist, based on my opinion of men and woman roles in the household. She didn't mean any harm by it, and I appreciated her honesty. She taught me to recognize stereotypes within myself and others and how damaging they can be.

During my middle school years, my grandmother was diagnosed with cancer. The summer prior to me going to high school is when she died.

Stephen Decatur High school was a challenge, but in my mind, I was ready for it. Freshman year, I played junior varsity football, but was not all that good because I truly didn't know all the positions. Many of my friends and peers had played since they were young kids in the Pop Warner league. I had only played in the backyard with friends and family. Although we went 10–0 that year, I didn't contribute much besides an extra body. It was good exposure, though, because it taught me early on how important camaraderie was among teammates. For some ill-advised reason, I attempted to take an advanced-level math course my freshman year. That was a bad idea; I failed it completely and didn't understand much at all. The teacher was no help, and his teaching style I didn't appreciate much. Years later I took a geometry course and barely passed. The main reason is that I didn't fully apply myself in high school and I didn't comprehend the importance of geometry. My favorite subjects were social studies and English, or what some call "integrated language arts."

I'll never forget Ms. Tillman's biology class. She seemed

to have the most patience with troubled students like myself. She was firm but fair, and she didn't sugarcoat her expectations. To pass her class you had to put forth a conscious effort to learn. I also have to mention Ms. Berquist. She was a nice teacher who used every effort to get students engaged in the learning environment.

One of the many mistakes that I made in high school was choosing to take French class instead of Spanish. I had no intention of going to Paris, but at the time I thought it was the right move. The teacher hated me, and I mean that literally. She would kick me out of her class for the littlest things. Granted, I take responsibility for being a class clown at times, which caused much of her dismay. I strongly believe she passed me with a D just to torment me for a second year.

There was one male teacher who spent most of his time pretending to be cool, as if he were auditioning for *Shaft*. Like the French teacher, Mr. Shaft would kick me out his class for the littlest gesture or response. Truly, I was a kid just trying to find my way and take it day by day.

I was not sure what I wanted to do after high school. I even failed a college research course because I didn't put forth the effort to submit any college applications. I thought I was already grown and didn't need school programs, or college for that matter, to motivate me.

My parents attended my high school graduation along with several of my aunts, uncles and cousins. I just wanted to walk across the stage without falling. Who knew it would take so long before last names with the letter *S* would be called? As I walked across the stage, I could feel my grandma watching me from above; she was very proud.

After graduation, I did what most high school graduates did—take a few family photos and then immediately head out to party with friends and celebrate. It was May 31, 2000, and after the parties ended, I had no plan in sight. I had taken the military ASVAB test to see if I had what it took to qualify to join the military.

My friend's dad, Butch, was a Navy recruiter, and he had the keen intellect to look at you and determine if you were qualified to be in the military. It was his belief that I didn't qualify and that I just wanted to be a street thug or bum, as he called it. I didn't know much about the Navy besides my uncle getting kicked out. I wanted to prove Butch wrong, just to show that I could pass the practice ASVAB as well as the actual ASVAB test. I hadn't given much thought to actually enlisting in the Navy. I knew my life had a purpose, but I just wasn't sure what it was yet.

CHAPTER 8

A FATHER S STRUGGLE: THE STORY OF FRANCIS

FRANCIS WILBERT SPENCE was a strange individual. He was loved by many and even worshipped by some. He was absent during my childhood, but over the years he became one of my closet friends and advisors. As a kid, I remember his brief stints in and out of jail for driving on a suspended license. Even when his license was revoked, he still insisted on driving. My dad was also jailed for failing to pay child support. By the time I was able to understand and have a relationship with him, I was a teenager. For as long as I could remember, poor Francis struggled with drug addiction, which gripped him throughout his life.

Pop, as most of the younger children in my family called him, usually found a new girlfriend as soon as he changed residences. What they saw in him, I'm not sure. He probably charmed his way into their lives and obscured what he had to offer. Sometimes upfront honesty similar to his goes along way. I do remember him taking me and my brother fishing once when we were kids. The boat started taking on water as soon as we left the shore.

My dad used to tell us stories of him playing basketball and football in high school. He said he was pretty good. My brother and I never really took the time to validate the information. We were just happy that he was proud to tell us about some of the good experiences in his life.

In his later years, his body started to deteriorate, beginning with his kidneys. As the years continued, he experienced heart problems and other ailments, which eventually led to having one of his legs amputated. I always felt like my dad was a friend I could talk to instead of a father. He had failed the being-a-father challenge during my childhood. I'm not sure what led him down the path of destruction, but over the years, using drugs was one of his main priorities. He tried to be a better father to Faren than he was to me and my brother. His fatherly instinct at least made him realize that he had to protect his daughter.

He stayed with my grandmother from time to time. When I was about seven or eight we disagreed on something and I tried punching him in the face. He choked and slammed me. That was the last time I tried that, and I planned to pay him back when I got older. On many occasions, my grandmother would put her house up as collateral to get him out of jail. His snoring could awake the dead, and once up, you could forget about trying to go back to sleep; it was nearly impossible. As a result of my dad's shortfalls, I knew no one could tell me what to do. I was the kid who was his own parent. I felt that I was smarter, and they didn't deserve the right to control anything I said or did.

It was hard watching my father's health decline at such a fast pace. He would go to dialysis treatment three days a week. When I was a child he weighed over 250 pounds, with a beer gut. We used to call him the "big beer can" due to the size of his stomach. Toward the end, he was barely eighty-five pounds, and partially restricted to a wheel chair. I felt somewhat sorry for him. A life of drug abuse will do that you. While he was living in a nursing home, I could still find him outside smoking cigarettes on a frigid winter night.

On one occasion, I went to pick him up and found him outside in a car with a young female; both appeared to be high off pot. He didn't let much slow him down. My dad was one of the few people I've known who could befriend complete strangers in minutes and then would become roommates with them within days. He fancied himself as somewhat of a comedian. My dad often asked my female friends if they would set him up on a date with their mothers, or whether they had single sisters. He was a very talented cook and could make almost anything from scratch—pizza, shrimp egg foo young, just to name a few. I would often have to remind him that the art of cooking started with washing his hands. This seemed to be a step he needed constant reminders of.

My dad and I worked together at Paul Revere Smorgasbord, a well-known buffet in Ocean City. The managers really liked him and he was able to work there off and on. For some odd reason, they employed him any summer he was willing to work. This particular summer, I was hired to be a cook for the buffet line. I would prep for the next day, monitor what needed to be cooked, and restock food in the warmers. It was really a brainless position; all you had to do was pay attention.

My dad worked directly behind me at a sink station, where he was tasked with washing pots and pans. It seemed that I was always busy and he was always on break, just relaxing and walking around socializing. One day I got fed up with it and asked him to switch positions. He agreed because it didn't matter to him; he had job security and he got paid the same. Unfortunately for me, he could not keep up with the demand for food. One of the assistant managers ordered me to return to the job for which I had been hired. I resented his tone, so I quit and walked out. I chalk that up to young adolescence. If I had been mature enough, I would have understood where the manager was coming from and returned to my regular, assigned duty. I blamed my father somewhat, but it was mostly my fault. I didn't have the authority to swap positions, and doing so hurt the business. You live and you learn. Needless to say, this was the last time my dad and I worked together.

December 5, 2014, my father passed away in

Wilmington, Delaware. He succumbed to the ailments that plagued him over twelve-plus years. I remember the phone call we shared on Thanksgiving that year. He asked me when I was coming home and I told him a few weeks before Christmas. His exact words were "That's a bet."

For years I thought that I was prepared for the day my father would die. The truth is, I was not. I got the call from my brother Keon around four in the morning. It was hard to believe and even harder to accept. My long-term friend and confidant was no longer among the living. If it hadn't been for the support of my family, I don't know how I could have dealt with the loss. We didn't have the best relationship, but I owed my father for bringing me into this world and for trying his best to make a positive impact on our friendship.

His funeral was held at the church I grew up in, Calvary United Methodist. This was also the church most of my family had attended at some point. If my memory serves me correctly, this was the first time I had set foot in this church since my grandmother's funeral in 1995. As I walked into the church, the pure presence of being there made me stronger. I had prepped a speech a few days before because I knew I had to say something in my dad's honor. It wouldn't have felt right to not say anything at all, knowing I would never get this opportunity again. Here is what I said:

"My dad was an inspiration to some and a temporary burden to others. He would befriend total strangers and would be considered family within minutes. When he got older and his health started to decline, he had this unusual way to make me and Keon feel like we were his parents and he was our child. No matter the rules we set or the things we told him not to do, he would listen during the conversation and proceed to do what he wanted after the conversation ended. We lost not a father but a good friend and advisor. I could say just about anything to him unfiltered. I'm going to miss you, old fellow. Rest assured that me, Keon, Faren and all the kids and family will be fine. Watch over us and make sure the demons of life don't get ahold of us. Be sure to tell Grandma, Aunt Ruth and Uncle Orphus that we love them and they will always be a part of our hearts. So many more to name, but by now my composure is starting to waiver. I'm crying typing this up. Love you, Pop."

Obituary for Francis W. Spence

Francis Wilbert Spence, affectionately known as "Frank" and "Uncle Gus," son of the late Cummings Purnell and Evelyn Spence, was born on June 12, 1956. He departed this life on Friday December 5, 2014 in Wilmington, Delaware. Francis attended Calvary United Methodist Church as a young adult, where he was an usher and a member of "The Mighty Voices." He was also a member of the Trinity AUMP Church in Northeast, Maryland, where he attended Bible study and sang in the choir. Francis loved the Lord. Francis received his early education at Cedar Chapel Grade School in Newark, Maryland, and also attended Stephen Decatur High School in Berlin, Maryland. He was involved in football and basketball, but especially loved playing football. Francis was previously employed at Paul Revere Smorgasbord (Plim Plaza) as a cook, and also had various jobs in the Ocean City surrounding area. Francis enjoyed crabbing, fishing, cooking, making people laugh and living life. He was always "the life of the party." Francis thought he was the best at playing Scrabble, Spades, Scattergories, and Yahtzee. If there was a game to be played, he would teach you how to play while cheating you at the same time. Francis had a smile that could warm anyone's heart. He loved his family unconditionally, and enjoyed family gatherings. Francis was preceded in death by his father, Cummings Francis Purnell, mother, Evelyn Iva Spence, brother George Spence, sister Ruth Reid, and brother Orphus Land. He leaves to cherish two sons; one daughter; three granddaughters; three grandsons; one brother; four sisters; and a host of nieces, nephews, great-nieces, great nephews, cousins, other relatives and close friends.

CHAPTER 9

MY MOTHER S STORY

MY MOTHER DIDN'T DISCUSS much about her childhood, except the fact that her mother, Virginia Crippen, suffered from some type of mental disability. Her mother often tormented her kids well past the point of child abuse, even flirting with the thought of ending their lives as kids. I never met my grandmother on my mom's side. I am not sure when or where she died. I often felt sad that I didn't know many siblings from my mom's side of the family. This may be due in part from me spending the majority of my childhood with my grandma.

My mom had my sister Konya when she was fifteen years old. Having a child at such a young age could be dramatic. I have often thought that my mother's giving birth so young played some role in her strained relationship with my sister.

The only child my mother raised was my brother Keon. My sister was predominantly raised by her father's mother.

One year, my mom decided she was going to be a chaperone for one of my school field trips to the zoo. I clearly remember that I didn't enjoy the trip at all. Here I was being chaperoned by a stranger, also known as my mother, who was trying to escort me and my classmates around the zoo. My friends seemed to like her, while I was trying to avoid her and minimize any interaction. A few years later, I came to realize that my mom had been dating the father of one of my friends. That was one of the reasons he grew so fond of her during the zoo trip. I made sure she never chaperoned another trip for the rest of my time in school.

Over the years growing up, I met my mom's brother and sisters: my aunts Coya, Carol, and Mona, and Uncle Clay. I try to keep in touch with some of their kids. Uncle Clay was an awkward individual. I used to witness him walking up and down the streets, going to and from the liquor store. He would work odd jobs and satisfy himself by drinking and smoking cigarettes. He didn't have any kids that I know off. Many people thought he was crazy because of the way he carried himself. He had a thick beard, and based on his appearance he was lacking in personal hygiene. Generally, he was a very nice person. Every time he saw me he knew who I was.

During my years as a toddler, my mom had a stroke. After her stroke, she suffered from epilepsy and walked with a severe limp. She always told my friends about how she took sick and how she learned how to walk and talk again. She often made them cry. Mom had a good heart but a strange way of showing it at times. Due to her disability, she only worked jobs such as grocery store cashier and caretaker jobs for the elderly.

Years ago, we both worked at a Pathmark grocery store. I was an overnight stocker and she was a cashier. It was pretty embarrassing for her to introduce me to all of her coworkers and store patrons while at work. I was so relieved when the manager put me on the overnight shift. Mom enjoyed grocery shopping for the elderly or just keeping them company. She once had a job at a casino, which was odd because she was an avid gambler. Lucky for her, the casino did not allow their employees to gamble at their place of employment. On her off days, she would drive about an hour away to another casino to satisfy her gambling fix. If she wasn't gambling, she was satisfying her obsession with Chesapeake Bay crabs. She would have been happy to eat crabs every day, all year round if she could. Mom would complain about driving long distances, day or night—except when it came to going somewhere to buy crabs or heading north to Atlantic City casinos. She would drive halfway around the world if the crabs were plump and cheap.

My brother Keon grew up with her, and I have to say I'm glad he did instead of me. I don't know how far I would have made it. During his early teenage years, I remember him and our mother would get into physical altercations, resulting in both being charged with assault. My brother was pretty laid-back at the time, but he would always stand up for himself. He had to endure a lot growing up, specifically my mom's five marriages. Each was short lived. Adapting to a new stepfather every couple of years had to be beyond challenging for Keon.

My brother was tall for his age, which worked out to his benefit. He often protected my mom from these men. She would task my brother to be her bodyguard in the midst of a spousal disagreement. I remember her telling us that her husbands, whoever they were at the time, came before her kids. This didn't make much sense to us then, and still does not make sense now. In my view, kids should always come first.

I am not sure if my mother chose to get married out of love or the simple, false belief that marriage would provide her security and stability. I did try living with her a few times, but it never lasted more than six months. I chose to move out for several reasons. On one occasion, she had moved to Delaware in a neighborhood called Brookmont Farms. Anyone that heard of this neighborhood knew it was a rough area, rife with crime and violence. I was in the house asleep one day and awoke to the sound of gunshots outside. This was one of the first instances in which I knew that I was out of my element and needed to get back to the country. It was clear that I would not evolve into the man I wanted to be under her roof.

Chapter 10

RELATIONSHIPS

I NEVER REALLY DISCUSSED with my father or mother how to treat a woman or how to behave in a relationship. The first and only lesson I received, from my older girl cousins, was that when you took a girl out to the movies or on a date, the guy was supposed to pay for everything. I followed that advice for many years. Through my teen years, I only had a few girlfriends, but I had a lot of girls that were friends.

Instead of using this chapter to detail all of my stories of romance, deception, heartbreaks or breaking hearts, I would like to focus on the things that I learned. Before you start a relationship, make sure you truly understand what you are getting yourself into. If a girl's parents don't like you or don't approve of your relationship with their daughter, you are bound for disaster.

Let's face the facts; not everyone wants their kids dating someone of the opposite race or ethnic background. On the other hand, some parents just want their kids to be happy. Hopefully, one day, all people will see past the skin color and truly evaluate a person based on their character.

One of my best friends in high school was a Caucasian female. It was a friendship without hidden agendas or expectations; we cared for each other strictly as friends. Occasionally, she would pick me up for school, and sometimes me, her and other friends would go to different places to hang out. She fell in love with one of my other close friends. I thought they made a great couple—you could sense the happiness they found in each other. What I didn't realize at the time was that my female best friend's Italian parents had a severe disdain for black people and strongly disapproved of their daughter dating a black guy. Furthermore, I suppose having black friends, or for that matter hanging out with them, was also frowned upon.

Growing up in an area that was predominantly white, we were taught not to judge people by the color of their skin. Everyone seemed to get along for the most part, but there were some small factions that were taught hatred at a young age. I tried not to let it bother me, but such overt prejudice was somewhat troubling.

In a relationship, you have to be fully committed to the other person and not be influenced by social dynamics outside of your relationship. In high school, there was a term called "puppy love." It simply meant young love not destined to last. Another useful lesson was not to start a new relationship if I was currently involved with another person. I was guilty of this. When you are young and narrow-minded you like to think you are keeping your options open.

Enjoy the good times and don't dwell on the bad. I made hundreds of mistakes in my relationships. Even though they occurred decades ago, they still bring back memories from time to time. You can't dwell in the past forever but you can make sure that your family and friends don't make the same mistakes. My longest childhood relationship ended when me and my girlfriend just grew apart. There was no ill-will towards one another; the split was both amicable and inevitable. I learned a lot in that relationship, and it exposed me to things that I would not have seen, such as the *Godfather* trilogy, which is still one of my favorite movie series. This was the start of my passion for mafia movies and films based on organized crime.

Listening to music also helped me a lot. Although I am an avid rap fan, I listen to a lot more rhythm and blues, traditionally called R&B. Through the ups and downs, the music kept me going. Even to this day, I could put on some '90s R&B and be completely relaxed and back in that element.

CHAPTER 11

THE ROAD TO SUCCESS

I HAD NO LONG-TERM plans in place after I got out of school. The year I graduated, many people thought the world would end in the year 2000. I didn't pay much attention to it; I was too busy hanging out with my so-called friends and family, and living the life of no responsibility. I struggled to maintain a stable job after high school. I usually worked hard for the summer and planned to take an easy job during the winter.

One year, my mom's newest husband, Bob, bought me a used car, a 1984 Saab. The car was an old, faded gray sedan with a manual transmission. I remember driving it off the lot and teaching myself how to shift, and, in the process, nearly tearing up all of the gears. I used to call the car a sob story because there was always something wrong with it. The fuel pump broke after a few months, which cost close to a thousand dollars to fix. After a while the brakes started to fail due to leaks from the master cylinder. The car problems continued to be complex and beyond my ability to repair.

Despite all the car problems, I piled up a stack of unpaid traffic tickets, which led to my license being suspended. I guess some of my father had rubbed off on me after all. On one occasion, I grew tired from waiting at an off-ramp traffic light. It felt as if I had been sitting there for at least five minutes and the light refused to change. As soon as I took matters into my own hands and drove through the red light with no traffic in sight, a police officer pulled me over. This simple lapse in judgment cost me about $310 in fines, and points on my license. After a certain number of points were accumulated your license would be suspended.

After going to court for driving on a suspended license, and spending seven days in jail, I realized that my life had a bigger purpose. I could no longer spend my days doing the bare minimum and not reaching my full potential. Two years prior, I had taken the ASVAB military evaluation test at the "encouragement" of my friend's father. I now believe that he used reverse psychology to make me believe that if I took the test, I wouldn't qualify. I think he saw potential within me but wouldn't openly admit to it.

I scored well on the test and had a chance to join the Navy right out of high school, but I wasn't quite sold on a life at sea. My uncle Skip was the only person in my family who had joined the Navy. His stories were mostly full of fluff or bad conduct. He often ended up in the brig, a military term for detention center or jail. He was proud of his service, and I remember a portrait of him in uniform hanging on his wall.

My cousins Shamica and Alfonso, whom I was staying with at the time, always looked out for me. They gave me a place to lay my head and gather my thoughts. I could always count on them to give me good advice and tell me exactly how it was, instead of what I wanted to hear. They encouraged me to do better and get away from the small-town setting. Even when my future was uncertain, they never rushed me to make a decision.

I spent one of my last free weekends with Keon. He gave me about a hundred bucks and wished me the best. A lot of my family and friends didn't think I would actually join the Navy—not because I couldn't do it, but for the simple fact that the military had rules and strict codes of conduct, and I didn't like abiding by rules.

My girlfriend at the time didn't want me to join the military and leave her. I tried to explain that I had dreams, and this was the path that I needed to follow to achieve them. I thought she of all people would understand, since she had been around for a while and witnessed my troubled lifestyle and poor decision-making. I didn't have the family structure that she had been raised with, but I knew enough to realize what my options were if I ever wanted to escape this small town.

On February 13, 2002, I enlisted in the Navy to support and defend my country against all enemies foreign and domestic. My journey in life was now just beginning!

CHAPTER 12

BOOT CAMP

GROWING UP, I NEVER had the opportunity to travel much. I would spend a summer or two in Washington, DC, with my cousins, and once we traveled to Hershey Park in Pennsylvania. As my departure date drew closer, I was transported to Baltimore to go to MEPS, as we all call it, also known as the Military Entrance Processing Station. The Navy placed delayed-entry program applicants in a hotel and provided a meal allowance to support us while away from home. During these few days, I was very nervous and uncertain of the journey ahead.

The MEPS station supported all military branches. The MEPS personnel decided whether you were physically and mentality capable of military service. The physical evaluation consisted of weird exercises, such as a duck-walk and other drills to determine if you had flat feet and so forth.

I still have not figured out how that process helps determine whether someone is a viable candidate for the military.

After going through these series of exercises and physical tests, I finally made it to the classifiers who determined which Navy ratings would be available for me. Initially, my first impression was that even the job classifiers didn't think I was cut out for the Navy and that I wouldn't last long. This was mostly in part to my conflicts with law enforcement and the corresponding paperwork that accompanied me from the recruiting station. I had to convince them that I was serious and dedicated to succeeding in the Navy.

The classifier informed me that there were two jobs that I could choose from—a cook or mess management specialist (MS), or a storekeeper (SK). I chose SK because I was fascinated with the idea of working in a warehouse and conducting inventory. This would be far different than anything that I was used to doing. A few days later, I was on an airplane headed to Chicago for further transport to Navy boot camp at Great Lakes, Illinois. This was also my first time flying on an airplane. I wasn't terrified at first, because I didn't know what to expect.

We received strict instructions to report to the airport United Service Organizations (USO) office upon our arrival. The USO provided food and refreshments while we waited for buses to take us to boot camp. The bus ride didn't seem that long, especially when you were enjoying the scenery and experiencing a world you had never seen. When we arrived to boot camp, the fun was over. We were greeted by drill sergeants, who came on the bus yelling at us to disembark and form a single-file line for processing. I wasn't used to someone yelling at me in such close proximity, but at this point I realized I was no longer in control and had to obey.

The first week of boot camp was known as your processing days, which were mostly called your "P" days. During this week, you went through a bunch of medical screenings, received about twenty vaccines, and received your uniforms and associated toiletries. One of the most memorable things about your first week in boot camp was the buzz haircut. There were no preferences; you got your hair trimmed off to the lowest setting possible on the electric clippers. There were no line ups or questions asked. You simply sat for a few minutes and the assembly line continued to move.

There was also a point during this week when you were threatened to disclose anything that your recruiter held out of your paperwork, or anything that he or she may have told you not to disclose. The boot camp personnel sternly warned you: If they found out anything that you hadn't disclosed, you could be separated any time prior to graduation. This led to a point where any and everyone was confessing to the littlest things, such as traffic tickets or smoking pot.

Boot camp typically lasted eight weeks, unless you got an assignment memorandum (ASMO) to another division that was weeks behind your current start date. For me, boot camp started off in the harsh February winter. There was snow everywhere, and it was extremely cold. I had not experienced this type of cold weather in Maryland. In boot camp, you were part of a division, in my case Division 163. You did everything together and marched from place to place around the base. You slept in the same compartments, on bunk beds, with about sixty other males. Division 163 was an integrated division, which meant we had both males and females. The males slept in one compartment and the females slept in the other one. I was our division's master-at-arms, which meant I was in charge of making sure that our berthing compartment and heads, which is a term for bathrooms, were cleaned. It was a tough job, but I was able to adapt and direct my fellow recruits on which areas needed to be cleaned. I was also responsible for ensuring that the males were properly accounted for and in a single-file line when departing our quarters to attend chow or other events, such as physical training and any destinations around the base.

During boot camp, you were required to be a third-class swimmer. This was indeed a challenge for me and, by the looks of it, a problem for the majority of African American recruits as well. We were instructed to swim while flat on our backs, and we had to tread water for five minutes. Sounds easy, right? It took me six and a half weeks to pass my swim test. I marched day in and day out to the pool with my towel in hand. I started to wonder what would happen if I didn't pass my swim test. Had my time in boot camp been all for nothing? How would my peers receive me if I returned to my hometown after failing boot camp for not being able to pass a swim test? I had to cast these fears aside and focus on the task at hand. God wouldn't have brought me this far to leave me, and wouldn't let me come all this way to fail. I passed my swim test by the grace of God and didn't look back. The only thing left was to graduate boot camp.

My boot camp graduation was a fabulous affair—lots of music, flags, and military honors throughout the ceremony. I had finished boot camp the same way I started, with no one in attendance and on my own. It didn't bother me seeing all my fellow graduates with their families. I was used to being alone. Next stop for me: Meridian, Mississippi.

CHAPTER 13

ROAD LESS TRAVELED

WHO COULD HAVE GUESSED that a wayward country boy from the Eastern Shore of Maryland would actually reform himself into a contributing member to society? If someone had told me sixteen years ago that I would, I would have told them to throw more coins into the wishing well.

After completing storekeeper apprenticeship school in Meridian, Mississippi, I headed to my first duty station in Marietta, Georgia. I had done so well that I was selected for accelerated advancement to paygrade E-4. My first duty station was VFA-203, a F/A-18 squadron. After being onboard for about six months, I was able to put on the petty officer third class, E-4 paygrade and assume a position of increased responsibility. When you receive a form of meritorious promotion, your increase in pay is effective immediately. Under normal circumstances, from an advancement exam you could possibly wait up to six months to receive your pay increase. I took the E-5 advancement exam later that year and met the final multiple score required for advancement to petty officer second class, paygrade E-5. My co-workers were just as shocked as I was when the advancement results came out.

At the time, I had been in the Navy a year and half. It was uncommon for sailors to advance this fast. I took it as a blessing and thanked the good Lord above. The squadron was scheduled to decommission the upcoming year, and I would have to negotiate orders to a new command. After two years in Marietta, Georgia, I headed to my next duty station at Naval Reserve Center, Roosevelt Roads, Puerto Rico. I originally had orders to go to a reserve center in Baltimore, but they were cancelled, and Puerto Rico was available. I never inquired as to why the orders were cancelled; I was excited for the opportunities that lay ahead. The only thing I knew about Puerto Rico was that Jennifer Lopez was from there. Who could argue with that? I didn't really take into consideration that the official language for Puerto Rico was Spanish and I didn't know any.

When I first arrived on the island and stopped by a McDonald's drive-through, that's when culture shock hit me—the menu was in Spanish. I spent three years in Puerto Rico and worked on the Roosevelt Roads base for about eight months. The reserve center relocated to Fort Buchanan and was later renamed a Navy operational support center. After three years of duty on the island, I was headed back to the mainland US for a tour in Virginia Beach, Virginia.

In Virginia, I was stationed on the Little Creek base at Navy Operational Support Team Two, which was later renamed SEAL Team 18. This is where I really started to define my role in the Navy, and I fully understood my responsibilities to support the warfighters and maintain a global force for good. At this command, I deployed to Iraq for forty-five days to support a US Customs mission. I was truly out of my element in the 120-degree Iraqi sun. In the special warfare community, there were no complaints; you simply adapted and overcame. I was able to attend a lot of training at this command and hone my weapons skills. During the tour, I was advanced to petty officer first class, paygrade E-6 from the advancement exam, and also earned my bachelor's degree in criminal justice.

So, how did I advance so fast? Two words: Hard work.

I started to feel like I had outgrown my billet assignment at the SEAL Team and accomplished a lot. In order to modify my duty assignment orders from four years to three, it was agreed that I would volunteer to take an individual augmentee (IA), or global support assignment (GSA), overseas.

Little did I know, there was no preference given in assignment. I received the phone call that I would be headed to Afghanistan for seven months, boots on ground. Initially I was shocked, based on all the attention Afghanistan was receiving. It seemed like there were bombings and terrorist attacks almost daily. Fortunately for me, the SEAL Team had prepared me mentally to accept all challenges head on, and imbued in me the belief that it was my duty to make the world a safer place regardless of what role I was to play.

I reported to Fort Jackson, South Carolina, for three weeks of combat training, which was led by Army instructors for all of the Navy sailors deploying to support an IA or GSA overseas. The training consisted of Humvee driving, range qualifications, land navigation, culture awareness, physical fitness, first aid, and so forth. We trained in our body armor and with our weapons like we were in country overseas.

We left South Carolina a few days after Thanksgiving for the long journey to Afghanistan. Being in a war zone is an experience you never forget. I don't share the stories because they are somewhat troubling. Only someone who served over there can relate. I would often ask God why I was still alive after attending multiple ceremonies on the airfield, saluting as deceased service members were loaded on planes headed to Dover Air Force Base. My time in Afghanistan ended in the summer of 2011. I negotiated a follow-on assignment to a ship out of Pearl Harbor, Hawaii.

The USS *Crommelin* was a frigate that held about 180 sailors. After being onboard for about six months, news came that the ship was going to be decommissioned. This tour of duty lasted less than two years, but I finally learned why so many Navy folks yearn for the ship life. Euphoria overcomes you when the ship is underway and you are surrounded by nothing but blue water. The team of sailors form close-knit bonds because we all have to depend on one another for survival. If a fire or flooding breaks out at sea, we must work together to save the ship.

My next assignment was in San Diego. I had been there several times over my career for various schools and conferences. This was my first time being stationed there. I was assigned to NAVSUP (Naval Supply) Global Logistics Support. This was traditionally a supply command that provided policy and oversight on all facets of managing supplies and services to the Navy and other branches of service. This is where I learned the full spectrum on how supply operations impacted the world and what tools we had at our disposal to respond to contingency operations and natural disasters.

After being at the command for almost a year, I was selected for advancement to chief petty officer. The following year, I earned a master's degree in business administration.

These achievements culminated a career founded on hard work and dedication, accepting challenging duty assignments and sustaining superior performance. Great mentors along the way molded and guided me to exceed expectations and reach my full potential.

The Navy saved me from my worst enemy—myself. I used my shortcomings as fuel to push me throughout my career to be the best I could be. If I had sat and complained about all the opportunities that I never had growing up, I would still be in a sunken place. Would my life have been different if my parents stayed married? What if my dad never got hooked on drugs? I can't control the answers to these questions, and I certainly cannot change what happened. What I can do is take advantage of the opportunities that I have been presented, and overcome my obstacles to become someone that my kids, nieces, nephews and family will be proud of. I know my grandmother and father are watching my every move. I never want to let them down.

ACKNOWLEDGMENTS

First and foremost, I would like to thank God for allowing me to be here. I would like to thank my family and friends for making my childhood and adult experiences worthwhile. Although we do not always keep in contact, we are forged together forever. The depictions in this book are not meant to discredit anyone. They simply illustrate the childhood foundation that formed me into the man I am today.

I started writing this book November 2, 2012, and finally got the focus and drive to finish it October 2017. So many things have changed throughout the draft of this book. I will vividly describe my military career and life experiences in the sequel to this book. To understand where my career goes from here, you must first understand where I came from.

ABOUT THE AUTHOR

Senior Chief Petty Officer Keshawn A. Spence was born in Salisbury, Maryland. Two years after graduating Stephen Decatur High School in Berlin, Maryland, he entered the United States Navy and began Basic Training in Great Lakes, IL in 2002.

Following Basic Training he completed Storekeeper (SK) "A" School at Naval Training Center, Meridian, MS. He reported to his first command VFA-203, in Marietta, Georgia from 2002-2004. His subsequent assignments include: Navy Operational Support Center, Puerto Rico (2004-2007), SEAL Team EIGHTEEN (2007-2010), ECRC FWD San Diego (2010-2011), USS CROMMELIN (FFG 37) (2011-2012), NAVSUP Global Logistics Support (2012-2014), USS CHAFEE (DDG 90) (2014-2016), and currently

Commander, Navy Air Force Reserve. Senior Chief Spence has completed three overseas deployments in Iraq (2009), Afghanistan (2010-2011), and a 2015 WESTPAC/Southern Seas deployment.

Keshawn Spence earned a bachelor's degree in criminal justice from Saint Leo University in May 2009, an MBA in human resource administration in 2014, and is a graduate of the Senior Enlisted Academy, Class 207 Red. His Navy qualifications include three warfare pins: Surface, Expeditionary, Aviation; and seven Navy Enlisted Classification codes.

His personal decorations include the Joint Service Commendation Medal, Navy and Marine Corps Commendation Medal, Navy and Marine Corps Achievement Medal (8th award), Military Outstanding Volunteer Service Medal, Good Conduct Medal (4 bronze stars), as well as other campaign and service awards.

CPSIA information can be obtained
at www.ICGtesting.com
Printed in the USA
BVHW06s0529010518
514824BV00033B/1043/P